Praying the Stations

Dedication

To my mother Elynor Lamkins, my first and best friend.
Love you forever, too.

A Reconciliation Service

As its title suggests, this way of the cross can be used as part of a reconciliation service for teens. "A Conversation Before the Crucifix" on page three can serve as the opening prayer. Each station has a Scripture reading and reflection, an examination of conscience ("Jesus asks"), and a personal act of sorrow (prayed at the end of each station by "all"). It takes approximately thirty minutes to complete the fourteen stations with a group. The last half hour of an hour-long reconciliation service can be used for individual confessions.

The Scripture passages contained herein are from the *New Revised Standard Version of the Bible*, copyright © 1989, by the Division of Christian Education of the National Council of Churches of Christ in the U.S.A. All rights reserved.

Twenty-Third Publications
A Division of Bayard
185 Willow Street
P.O. Box 180
Mystic, CT 06355
(860) 536-2611
(800) 321-0411

© Copyright 2001 Colleen D. Rainone. All rights reserved. No part of this publication may be reproduced in any manner without prior written permission of the publisher. Write to the Permissions Editor.

ISBN:1-58595-124-2
Printed in the U.S.A.

A Conversation Before the Crucifix

All Jesus, we come here before you with so many questions, doubts, and even fears about life in general and about our own lives in particular. We don't even know how to talk to you because you are the most puzzling question of all. You lived on earth such a long time ago, and you were such a good and unselfish person. So it would seem that we have absolutely nothing in common. Yet, for some reason we are here, and in some mysterious way you are here, too.

Please speak to our hearts and help us to understand how you relate to us and what you can teach us about ourselves and our dealings with others.

Leader My friends, as you walk with me on this way of the cross, you will be amazed at just how much we have in common.

I do know that growing up is difficult. Even though some of my friends were far from perfect, I could be friends with them without imitating them or going against my conscience. Perhaps this is where we're different and where I can help you understand yourself better.

My friends were very important to me, as yours are to you. Friends have a powerful influence on our lives. As much as I loved my friends, I knew that they had faults, some of which caused me a lot of pain. However, I knew that my happiness could not depend entirely on their acceptance or loyalty, but on being true to myself and true to what I knew to be right. So even when my friends disagreed with me or betrayed me, I continued to love them and forgive them. This wasn't easy for me.

As difficult as it is to forgive people who have wronged you, it is even harder to ask for forgiveness because you first have to admit that you did something wrong. As you make your way through the fourteen stations, remember the words I taught you in the Our Father: "Forgive us our trespasses as we forgive those who trespass against us."

Those who do well at school get picked on by their peers while others become popular because they are cool and
willing to break a few rules.

First Station

Leader Jesus is condemned to death.

All We adore you, Jesus, and we thank you; because by your holy cross you have redeemed us and our friends.

Reader 1 Pilate said to them, "Who do you want me to release for you..." And they said, "Barabbas" [a rebel and murderer]. Pilate said to them, "Then what should I do with Jesus who is called the Messiah?" All of them said, "Let him be crucified!" Then he asked, "Why, what evil has he done?" But they shouted all the more, "Let him be crucified!" (Matthew 27:17, 21–23).

Reader 2 What's wrong with this picture? How could people sentence a completely innocent man to death? They would rather allow the popular "cool" guy to get away with murder than to allow Jesus to continue doing good. Actually, it's really not so hard to imagine. We do this all the time on a smaller scale. For example, those who do well at school get picked on by their peers while others become popular because they are cool and willing to break a few rules. We have much to learn from Jesus.

Leader Jesus asks: How did you feel the last time you got teased for doing something good? *(pause)* Have you ever picked on anyone for being good? *(pause)* Do you act tough so that your friends will think you're cool? *(pause)*

All Jesus, as much as I dislike being picked on for doing well or being good, I know there have been times when I have picked on others just to be accepted by them or to avoid ridicule. I know that this is cowardly. Forgive me, please. Help me to do what is right and to forgive those who make fun of me for doing the right thing. Thank you for loving me so much. Amen.

Even when we are guilty
of some wrongdoing,
we still argue, make excuses,
or complain about the type
of punishment we receive.

Second Station

Leader   Jesus accepts his cross.

All   We adore you, Jesus, and we thank you; because by your holy cross you have redeemed us and our friends.

Reader 1   But he was wounded for our transgressions, crushed for our iniquities; upon him was the punishment that made us whole, and by his bruises we are healed. He was oppressed, and he was afflicted, yet he did not open his mouth (Isaiah 53:5, 7).

Reader 2   Jesus just stood there and took it. Does this mean he was a wimp for not defending himself or putting up a fight? No, it means he is the truest friend we will ever have. Would you call a friend who takes the blame for something you did a wimp? Jesus took the blame for us even though it cost him his life. "That's not fair!" would probably be our response to being punished unfairly. Even when we are guilty of some wrongdoing, we still argue, make excuses, or complain about the type of punishment we receive. We have much to learn from Jesus.

Leader   Jesus asks: When someone gets blamed for something you did, do you have the courage to own up to the mistake? *(pause)* When you do get caught for doing something wrong, do you face the punishment without complaint or argument? *(pause)*

All   Jesus, for the times I have let others get in trouble because of me, forgive me. Help me to accept my punishment without talking back to my parents or teachers. Forgive those who accuse me unfairly or blame me for their problems. Thank you for loving me so much. Amen.

One bad play in a game or one bad grade on a report card can seem like the end of the world.

Third Station

Leader Jesus falls the first time.

All We adore you, Jesus, and we thank you; because by your holy cross you have redeemed us and our friends.

Reader 1 I gave my back to those who struck me... I did not hide my face from insult and spitting. The Lord God helps me; therefore I have not been disgraced; therefore I have set my face like flint, and I know that I shall not be put to shame (Isaiah 50:6–7).

Reader 2 It was bad enough that Jesus was condemned to die, but to fall flat on his face in front of a huge crowd! How humiliating! The mocking crowd might have thought him a failure, but that didn't stop him from finishing what he had to do because he knew that God was with him every step of the way. We, too, know how difficult it is to keep going after we have failed in something, especially when others make fun of us or tell us that we are no good. We even get the urge to quit. One bad play in a game or one bad grade on a report card can seem like the end of the world. But when we have someone cheering us on, despite our mistakes, we feel more confident to keep trying. We have much to learn from Jesus.

Leader Jesus asks: Do you make fun of others when they make a mistake, calling them "loser" or some other hurtful name? *(pause)* Do you quit just because others think you're a failure? *(pause)*

All Jesus, I am sorry for the times I have just given up because of what others have said about me. Forgive me also for the times I have put people down for their mistakes, and forgive those who do the same to me. Help me to build others up rather than tear them down. Thank you for loving me so much. Amen.

We tend to complain about our parents and their methods of discipline far more often than we say "thank you" when they do something nice for us.

Fourth Station

Leader   Jesus meets his mother.

All   We adore you, Jesus, and we thank you; because by your holy cross you have redeemed us and our friends.

Reader 1   When Jesus saw his mother and the disciple whom he loved standing beside her [near the cross], he said to his mother, "Woman, here is your son." Then he said to his disciple, "Here is your mother." And from that hour the disciple took her into his own home (John 19:26–27).

Reader 2   Jesus put his own pain aside, as great as it was, to care for his mother. After all, this was the woman who had made so many sacrifices for him. How easy it is for us to forget or ignore the sacrifices our parents have made from our infancy until now: the nightime feedings, the endless diapers, sleepless nights when we were sick, driving us everywhere we needed to go, and consoling us during every crisis. We tend to complain about them and their methods of discipline far more often than we say "thank you" when they do something nice for us. We have much to learn from Jesus.

Leader   Jesus asks: When was the last time you showed your gratitude to your parents? *(pause)* Can you think of some ways that you have shown disrespect to your parents and how you can make it up to them? *(pause)*

All   Jesus, I am sorry for the times I have been disrespectful to my parents. Teach me how to show my gratitude more often. Help me to forgive my parents when they overlook my good efforts or lose patience with me. Help me to love them as you loved your mother Mary. Thank you for loving me so much. Amen.

All of us need help from time to time, especially when we are going through a tough time.

Fifth Station

Leader Simon helps Jesus carry the cross.

All We adore you, Jesus, and we thank you; because by your holy cross you have redeemed us and our friends.

Reader 1 As they went out, they came upon a man from Cyrene named Simon; they compelled this man to carry his cross (Matthew 27:32).

Reader 2 This small gesture of Simon's must have been a great relief to Jesus. Though Jesus was the Son of God he was also fully human, and he felt the pain and agony of carrying the heavy cross. All of us need help from time to time, especially when we are going through a tough time. Yet how difficult it is for us to ask for help, and from the right people. On the one hand, we're afraid to turn to our parents, teachers, or advisors, because we think they "won't understand." Or maybe we think "they'll just give me a lecture." On the other hand, the friends to whom we readily vent our troubles can't always give us the help we really need. We have much to learn from Jesus.

Leader Jesus asks: Do you trust those with experience and maturity to guide you through difficult situations or do you try to handle everything on your own? *(pause)* Do you truly want to be helped or do you just want to complain about your troubles? *(pause)*

All Jesus, I prefer to turn to my friends when I have a problem because they listen to me. Even though I know they can't always help me, I feel better. Still, forgive me for the times I have misjudged my parents, teachers, and advisors by believing that they won't listen or don't care. Help me to keep an open mind about their advice and to forgive them when they misjudge my actions or intentions. Thank you for loving me so much. Amen.

Television, movies, and videos
give us false images of what
people should look like
and how they should act.
We strive to achieve this "look"
to perfection.

Sixth Station

Leader   Veronica wipes the face of Jesus.

All   We adore you, Jesus, and we thank you; because by your holy cross you have redeemed us and our friends.

Reader 1   He was despised and rejected by others; a man of suffering and acquainted with infirmity; and as one from whom others hide their faces he was despised, and we held him of no account (Isaiah 53:3).

Reader 2   In short, Jesus looked so disfigured and ugly, no one wanted to look at him or be near him. He was mocked and rejected by the "in crowd" of his day. Veronica didn't care what they said; she saw through Jesus' appearance to his true beauty and treated him with compassion. Television, movies, and videos give us false images of what people should look like and how they should act. We strive to achieve this "look" to perfection. We also judge others when they fail to do so. We poke fun at the kid with bad acne, the "slow" kid, those who are not good at sports, those who are heavy, or anyone who is considered unattractive for whatever reason. We have a lot to learn from Veronica's love and compassion. We have much to learn from Jesus.

Leader   Jesus asks: Have you mocked people for the way they look, walk, talk, or for any disabilities they might have? *(pause)* How do you feel when people tease you about your appearance or avoid being with you because of it? *(pause)*

All   Jesus, I dread it when my peers make fun of the way I look or act. Forgive them when they are cruel to me or to my friends. And forgive me, please, for the times I have made fun of or avoided the company of others. Help me to accept others as they are, as I would like to be accepted. Thank you for loving me so much. Amen.

We get so lost in everyday petty arguments and rivalries, as if our entire lives depend on winning these mini-battles.

Seventh Station

Leader Jesus falls a second time.

All We adore you, Jesus, and we thank you; because by your holy cross you have redeemed us and our friends.

Reader 1 And the people stood by, watching; but the leaders scoffed at him, saying, "He saved others; let him save himself if he is the Messiah of God, his chosen one!" (Luke 23:35).

Reader 2 How typical! A few loudmouths sway public opinion while the silent majority stand around and gawk. If Jesus had accepted their dare at that moment, he would have only risen from a fall. Instead he chose to give his life completely so that he and all of us could be raised to new life. We get so lost in everyday petty arguments and rivalries, as if our entire lives depend on winning these mini-battles. And why? We may think that being popular is more important than being true to ourselves. Sometimes we feel that we can't be happy with who we are unless others think well of us, too. Yet, the stronger person is the one who turns down these temptations to win the greater victory. We have much to learn from Jesus.

Leader Jesus asks: Do you allow yourself to be provoked into "proving yourself"? *(pause)* Do you let the opinion of others dictate how you behave? *(pause)*

All Jesus, I get so mad at myself when I let others get to me and provoke me to do things I wouldn't do otherwise. I wish I wasn't so easily persuaded. Forgive me for trying to be something I am not, and help me to see every day that my life is worth more than the shallow view others have of me. Thank you for loving me so much. Amen.

When we make a judgment
about someone based on gossip
and shun his or her company as
a result, it rarely occurs to us
that we could be denying
ourselves the best friend
we ever had.

Eighth Station

Leader Jesus speaks to the women.

All We adore you, Jesus, and we thank you; because by your holy cross you have redeemed us and our friends.

Reader 1 A great number of the people followed him, and among them were women who were beating their breasts and wailing for him. But Jesus turned to them and said, "Daughters of Jerusalem, do not weep for me but weep for yourselves and for your children" (Luke 23:27–28).

Reader 2 Some of these women were sincere in their sorrow for Jesus, but others were not. The sincere women knew Jesus personally and truly loved him; the insincere women knew about him through hearsay and they cried because everyone else was doing it. The insincere women eventually lost out because they never got to know Jesus or his teaching. When we make a judgment about someone based on gossip and shun his or her company as a result, it rarely occurs to us that we could be denying ourselves the best friend we ever had. What's more, the "friend" who hardly knows us isn't a true friend at all. We have much to learn from Jesus.

Leader Jesus asks: Have you ever hurt someone's reputation through gossip? *(pause)* Do you avoid people because of what you have heard through gossip, or do you try to get to know them personally, despite what your friends say? *(pause)*

All Jesus, I know how it feels when people talk about me behind my back, and I don't like it. Yet, I know I have been guilty of doing the same thing to others. Please forgive me as I forgive those who hurt me through gossip. May I learn to be a true friend by imitating and loving you. Thank you for loving me so much. Amen.

Sometimes our classmates,
and even our friends,
may pressure us to do things
we know are wrong, like drinking
alcohol, doing drugs, swearing,
or engaging in sexual acts.

Ninth Station

Leader Jesus falls a third time.

All We adore you, Jesus, and we thank you; because by your holy cross you have redeemed us and our friends.

Reader 1 Surely he has borne our infirmities and carried our diseases; yet we accounted him stricken, struck down by God, and afflicted (Isaiah 53:4).

Reader 2 No matter how hard the soldiers whipped him, no matter how much the crowd taunted him, Jesus kept getting up. He knew what he had to do, and he would do it no matter what pressure people put on him. Sometimes our classmates, and even our friends, may pressure us to do things we know are wrong, like drinking alcohol, doing drugs, swearing, or engaging in sexual acts. They tell us that everyone else is doing it, when in fact very few are doing it. They just want us to join them so they won't feel so alone or guilty. They won't admit that they were also pressured into their "first time." We need to let them know that we're not "everyone." Rather, we are someone who stands on his or her own feet. We have much to learn from Jesus.

Leader Jesus asks: Have you given into peer pressure and experimented with alcohol, drugs, or sexual acts? *(pause)* Do you swear or use profanity in order to be cool? *(pause)*

All Jesus, the pressure I put on myself at school or with my friends can be pretty hard to deal with at times. Help me to be strong. Forgive me for the times I have pressured others to go against their conscience, and forgive those who attempt to pressure me into doing the wrong thing. Thank you for loving me so much. Amen.

For the sake of fitting in, we allow advertisers and peers to tell us what kind of clothes, cosmetics, and other trendy products to wear.

Tenth Station

Leader Jesus is stripped of his garments.

All We adore you, Jesus, and we thank you; because by your holy cross you have redeemed us and our friends.

Reader 1 And when they had crucified him, they divided his clothes among themselves by casting lots [gambling]; then they sat down there and kept watch over him (Matthew 27:35–36).

Reader 2 What a humiliation for Jesus: to be stripped naked for everyone to see. How would we feel if this happened to us? As it is, we're already extremely self-conscious about the changes occurring in our bodies and how we appear to others. None of us would want to be exposed in public. Yet, ironically, we think nothing of watching other people expose themselves on TV, in movies, or in magazines. For the sake of fitting in, we allow advertisers and peers to tell us what kind of clothes, cosmetics, and other trendy products to wear. We're so obsessed with looking like everyone else that we are unable to see our own uniqueness and beauty. We have much to learn from Jesus.

Leader Jesus asks: In what ways do you show respect for your own body? Do you make sure that your boyfriend or girlfriend respects your body, too? *(pause)* Do you let others influence your choices about what to wear and how to act? *(pause)*

All Jesus, I get so worked up over how I look and what others think of me that I lose sight of the "me" inside, the me my parents love and you love. My need to be liked by peers is so strong sometimes that I am willing to watch what they watch or wear what they wear, even if it is wrong, even if I can't afford it. Forgive me, Jesus, and forgive them, too. Help me be true to myself. Thank you for loving me so much. Amen.

We sometimes insult people by attaching "labels" to them, sometimes just because they are different. We have much to learn from Jesus.

Eleventh Station

Leader Jesus is nailed to the cross.

All We adore you, Jesus, and we thank you; because by your holy cross you have redeemed us and our friends.

Reader 1 It was nine o'clock in the morning when they crucified him. The inscription of the charge against him read, "The King of the Jews" (Mark 15:25–26).

Reader 2 The Romans placed this inscription above Jesus' head, not as an affirmation of his true kingship but as an intentional insult against the Jews. We all have a way of insulting people by attaching labels to them, sometimes just because they are different. Yet, none of us likes being the target of such labels. Even when said in jest, these names can still hurt us, though we may not show it. At other times labeling can start fights that may cause someone to get hurt or even killed. We have much to learn from Jesus.

Leader Jesus asks: When you call someone a hurtful name, do you apologize afterwards? *(pause)* Do you try to reflect before you speak, especially when you are angry with someone? *(pause)*

All Jesus, it's true. Before I realize what I'm saying I blurt out a hurtful name. Forgive me and forgive those who call me names. Help me to focus on you at that moment when you hung upon the cross in great pain and with much sorrow. May I learn to call you my savior and may you always be the king of my heart. Thank you for loving me so much. Amen.

Some deaths seem senseless and unacceptable to us, like those that result from a violent shooting of high school students or a sudden accident.

Twelfth Station

Leader Jesus dies on the cross.

All We adore you, Jesus, and we thank you; because by your holy cross you have redeemed us and our friends.

Reader 1 Then Jesus, crying with a loud voice, said, "Father, into your hands I commend my spirit." Having said this, he breathed his last. When the centurion saw what had taken place, he praised God and said, "Certainly this man was innocent" (Luke 23:46–47).

Reader 2 Many people didn't even begin to understand Jesus' life or death until after he was raised from the dead. Until that moment his death seemed to be a senseless waste of a good life. Some deaths we can understand and accept, like the death of an elderly person. Yet other deaths seem senseless and unacceptable, like those that result from a violent shooting of high school students or a sudden accident. Yet it is only after the victims are gone that we realize just how valuable their lives were. Often great things are born from the ashes of these tragedies; for example, memorial foundations give life and opportunities to hundreds and thousands of people who would not have been able to receive help otherwise. We have much to learn from Jesus.

Leader Jesus asks: How do you show your appreciation of your family, friends, teachers, classmates, and acquaintances? *(pause)* Do you pray for them and for peace in your family and school? *(pause)*

All Jesus, if I had to face the sudden death of someone I really care about, I don't know how I could bear it. Forgive me for the times I take my family, friends, teachers, and classmates for granted. Help me to forgive them when it seems they take me for granted. Thank you for loving me so much. Amen.

Sometimes our friends let us down by failing to keep a promise, by preferring other people's company to ours, or by just not being there when we need them.

Thirteenth Station

Leader   Jesus is taken down from the cross.

All   We adore you, Jesus, and we thank you; because by your holy cross you have redeemed us and our friends.

Reader 1   After these things, Joseph of Arimathea, who was a disciple of Jesus, though a secret one because of his fear of the Jews, asked Pilate to let him take away the body of Jesus. Pilate gave him permission; so he came and removed his body (John 19:38).

Reader 2   While Jesus lived on earth, Joseph didn't want his peers, who despised Jesus, to know that he really liked and respected him. Imperfect as he was, Joseph was still Jesus' friend right to the end. Sometimes our friends let us down by failing to keep a promise, by preferring other people's company to ours, or by just not being there when we need them. They're not perfect, and neither are we. We need to be patient with each other's failings and appreciate the times they are there for us. We have much to learn from Jesus.

Leader   Jesus asks: Do you accept your friends' faults and failings, even when they cause you pain? *(pause)* Are you in turn the best friend you can be? *(pause)*

All   Jesus, forgive my friends when they let me down. I know that I need to be forgiven, too, for the times I have done the same to them. Help me to be the kind of friend you are to me. Thank you for loving me so much. Amen.

Are you willing to give up your favorite TV show or some other favorite activity to do a favor for a friend, a family member, or for a charitable cause?

Fourteenth Station

Leader Jesus is placed in the tomb.

All We adore you, Jesus, and we thank you; because by your holy cross you have redeemed us and our friends.

Reader 1 So Joseph took the body and wrapped it in a clean linen cloth and laid it in his own new tomb, which he had hewn in the rock. He then rolled a great stone to the door of the tomb and went away (Matthew 27:59–60).

Reader 2 For Joseph no act of kindness was too great for his friend. He gave over his new tomb, his most sacred piece of property. We're usually good at sharing our things. Yet, there's one thing we're not always willing to give up and share; and that's our time. Sometimes our time is more important to us than our possessions. We can always get new possessions, but we can't get time back. When we do a favor for someone, we give up an opportunity to spend our time the way we prefer. And yet, as Joseph shows, this is the mark of true friendship. We have much to learn from Jesus.

Leader Jesus asks: Are you willing to give up your favorite TV show or some other favorite activity to do a favor for a friend, a family member, or for a charitable cause? *(pause)* What acts of kindness have you shown to your family and friends lately? *(pause)*

All Jesus, sometimes I can be pretty stingy with my time without realizing it. I'm sorry for being selfish. Please forgive me as I forgive others when they are selfish with me. Thank you for loving me so much. Amen.

Parting Words from Jesus

Leader My friends, you see,
I do understand your struggles,
and I want to help you
work through them.
I hope that this time together
has helped you to remember
and think about what is important.
Know that I am always with you,
right in your heart.
I know how hard you try
to be the best you can be.
I listen; I care; I love you,
no matter what.